IT'S VACATION TIME!

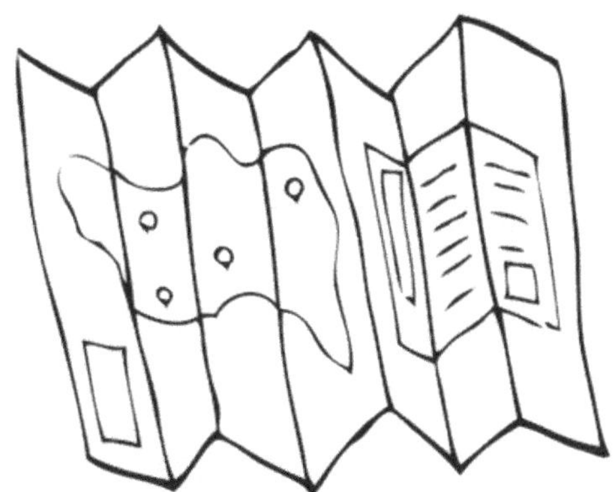

Use this journal to record the memories you make during vacations.

With different pages on vacation planning, journal writing, exploration reports, scrapbooking and sketching, you can always come back to your vacation memories even after the adventure is over!

VACATION PLANNING

PLACES I WANT TO SEE	THINGS I WANT TO DO	FOOD I WANT TO EAT

VACATION PLANNING

I've always wanted to...

in the exciting place called...

I will bring these stuff with me:

We will travel by:

People and pets who will be with me:

When do you want to go on this trip?

Draw a picture of what you want to do in your vacation:

VACATION PLANNING

I've always wanted to...

in the exciting place called...

I will bring these stuff with me:

People and pets who will be with me:

We will travel by:

When do you want to go on this trip?

Draw a picture of what you want to do in your vacation:

VACATION PLANNING

I've always wanted to...

in the exciting place called...

I will bring these stuff with me:

- [ ]
- [ ]
- [ ]
- [ ]
- [ ]

People and pets who will be with me:

- [ ]
- [ ]
- [ ]
- [ ]
- [ ]

We will travel by:

When do you want to go on this trip?

Draw a picture of what you want to do in your vacation:

VACATION PLANNING

I've always wanted to...

in the exciting place called...

I will bring these stuff with me:

-
-
-
-
-

People and pets who will be with me:

-
-
-
-
-

We will travel by:

When do you want to go on this trip?

Draw a picture of what you want to do in your vacation:

VACATION PLANNING

I've always wanted to...

in the exciting place called...

I will bring these stuff with me:

- [ ]
- [ ]
- [ ]
- [ ]
- [ ]

People and pets who will be with me:

- [ ]
- [ ]
- [ ]
- [ ]
- [ ]

We will travel by:

When do you want to go on this trip?

Draw a picture of what you want to do in your vacation:

VACATION PLANNING

I've always wanted to...

in the exciting place called...

I will bring these stuff with me:

- [ ]
- [ ]
- [ ]
- [ ]
- [ ]

People and pets who will be with me:

- [ ]
- [ ]
- [ ]
- [ ]
- [ ]

We will travel by:

When do you want to go on this trip?

Draw a picture of what you want to do in your vacation:

VACATION PLANNING

I've always wanted to...

in the exciting place called...

I will bring these stuff with me:

- [ ]
- [ ]
- [ ]
- [ ]
- [ ]

People and pets who will be with me:

- [ ]
- [ ]
- [ ]
- [ ]
- [ ]

We will travel by:

When do you want to go on this trip?

Draw a picture of what you want to do in your vacation:

VACATION PLANNING

I've always wanted to...

in the exciting place called...

I will bring these stuff with me:

- ☐
- ☐
- ☐
- ☐
- ☐

People and pets who will be with me:

- ☐
- ☐
- ☐
- ☐
- ☐

We will travel by:

When do you want to go on this trip?

Draw a picture of what you want to do in your vacation:

VACATION PLANNING

I've always wanted to...

in the exciting place called...

I will bring these stuff with me:

People and pets who will be with me:

We will travel by:

When do you want to go on this trip?

Draw a picture of what you want to do in your vacation:

VACATION PLANNING

I've always wanted to...

in the exciting place called...

I will bring these stuff with me:

We will travel by:

People and pets who will be with me:

When do you want to go on this trip?

Draw a picture of what you want to do in your vacation:

VACATION PLANNING

I've always wanted to...

in the exciting place called...

I will bring these stuff with me:

- [ ]
- [ ]
- [ ]
- [ ]
- [ ]

People and pets who will be with me:

- [ ]
- [ ]
- [ ]
- [ ]
- [ ]

We will travel by:

When do you want to go on this trip?

Draw a picture of what you want to do in your vacation:

VACATION PLANNING

I've always wanted to...

in the exciting place called...

I will bring these stuff with me:

- [ ]
- [ ]
- [ ]
- [ ]
- [ ]

People and pets who will be with me:

- [ ]
- [ ]
- [ ]
- [ ]
- [ ]

We will travel by:

When do you want to go on this trip?

Draw a picture of what you want to do in your vacation:

VACATION PLANNING

I've always wanted to...

in the exciting place called...

I will bring these stuff with me:

We will travel by:

People and pets who will be with me:

When do you want to go on this trip?

Draw a picture of what you want to do in your vacation:

VACATION PLANNING

I've always wanted to...

in the exciting place called...

I will bring these stuff with me:

We will travel by:

People and pets who will be with me:

When do you want to go on this trip?

Draw a picture of what you want to do in your vacation:

VACATION PLANNING

I've always wanted to...

in the exciting place called...

I will bring these stuff with me:

People and pets who will be with me:

We will travel by:

When do you want to go on this trip?

Draw a picture of what you want to do in your vacation:

VACATION PLANNING

I've always wanted to...

in the exciting place called...

I will bring these stuff with me:

-
-
-
-
-

People and pets who will be with me:

-
-
-
-
-

We will travel by:

When do you want to go on this trip?

Draw a picture of what you want to do in your vacation:

VACATION PLANNING

I've always wanted to...

in the exciting place called...

I will bring these stuff with me:

- [ ]
- [ ]
- [ ]
- [ ]
- [ ]

People and pets who will be with me:

- [ ]
- [ ]
- [ ]
- [ ]
- [ ]

We will travel by:

When do you want to go on this trip?

Draw a picture of what you want to do in your vacation:

VACATION PLANNING

I've always wanted to...

in the exciting place called...

I will bring these stuff with me:

-
-
-
-
-

People and pets who will be with me:

-
-
-
-
-

We will travel by:

When do you want to go on this trip?

Draw a picture of what you want to do in your vacation:

VACATION PLANNING

I've always wanted to...

in the exciting place called...

I will bring these stuff with me:

- ☐
- ☐
- ☐
- ☐
- ☐

People and pets who will be with me:

- ☐
- ☐
- ☐
- ☐
- ☐

We will travel by:

When do you want to go on this trip?

Draw a picture of what you want to do in your vacation:

VACATION PLANNING

I've always wanted to...

in the exciting place called...

I will bring these stuff with me:

We will travel by:

People and pets who will be with me:

When do you want to go on this trip?

Draw a picture of what you want to do in your vacation:

VACATION PLANNING

I've always wanted to...

in the exciting place called...

I will bring these stuff with me:

People and pets who will be with me:

We will travel by:

When do you want to go on this trip?

Draw a picture of what you want to do in your vacation:

VACATION PLANNING

I've always wanted to...

in the exciting place called...

I will bring these stuff with me:

We will travel by:

People and pets who will be with me:

When do you want to go on this trip?

Draw a picture of what you want to do in your vacation:

VACATION PLANNING

I've always wanted to...

in the exciting place called...

I will bring these stuff with me:

People and pets who will be with me:

We will travel by:

When do you want to go on this trip?

Draw a picture of what you want to do in your vacation:

VACATION PLANNING

I've always wanted to...

in the exciting place called...

I will bring these stuff with me:

- ☐
- ☐
- ☐
- ☐
- ☐

People and pets who will be with me:

- ☐
- ☐
- ☐
- ☐
- ☐

We will travel by:

When do you want to go on this trip?

Draw a picture of what you want to do in your vacation:

VACATION PLANNING

I've always wanted to...

in the exciting place called...

I will bring these stuff with me:

People and pets who will be with me:

We will travel by:

When do you want to go on this trip?

Draw a picture of what you want to do in your vacation:

VACATION PLANNING

I've always wanted to...

in the exciting place called...

I will bring these stuff with me:

We will travel by:

People and pets who will be with me:

When do you want to go on this trip?

Draw a picture of what you want to do in your vacation:

VACATION PLANNING

I've always wanted to...

in the exciting place called...

I will bring these stuff with me:

People and pets who will be with me:

We will travel by:

When do you want to go on this trip?

Draw a picture of what you want to do in your vacation:

VACATION PLANNING

I've always wanted to...

in the exciting place called...

I will bring these stuff with me:

- ☐ __________________________
- ☐ __________________________
- ☐ __________________________
- ☐ __________________________
- ☐ __________________________

People and pets who will be with me:

- ☐ __________________________
- ☐ __________________________
- ☐ __________________________
- ☐ __________________________
- ☐ __________________________

We will travel by:

When do you want to go on this trip?

Draw a picture of what you want to do in your vacation:

VACATION PLANNING

I've always wanted to...

in the exciting place called...

I will bring these stuff with me:

People and pets who will be with me:

We will travel by:

When do you want to go on this trip?

Draw a picture of what you want to do in your vacation:

VACATION PLANNING

I've always wanted to...

in the exciting place called...

I will bring these stuff with me:

-
-
-
-
-

People and pets who will be with me:

-
-
-
-
-

We will travel by:

When do you want to go on this trip?

Draw a picture of what you want to do in your vacation:

VACATION PLANNING

I've always wanted to...

in the exciting place called...

I will bring these stuff with me:

- [ ]
- [ ]
- [ ]
- [ ]
- [ ]

People and pets who will be with me:

- [ ]
- [ ]
- [ ]
- [ ]
- [ ]

We will travel by:

When do you want to go on this trip?

Draw a picture of what you want to do in your vacation:

JOURNAL WRITING

MY VACATION IN...

OVERALL RATING:

Tell us a story abour your vacation. WHEN did you go on your trip? WHERE did you visit? WHO were you with? WHAT did you do?

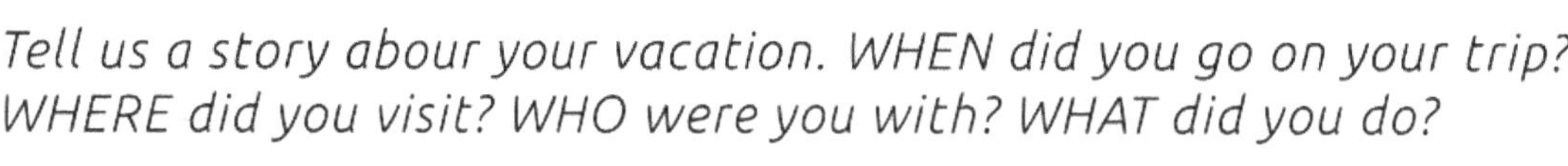

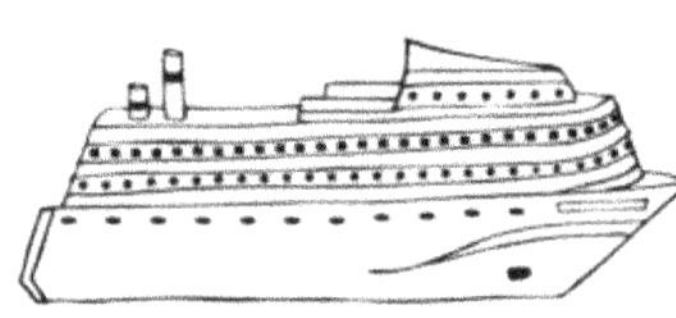  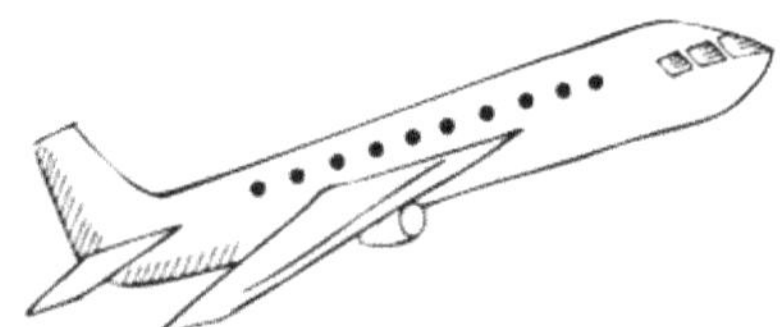

MY EXPLORATION REPORT:

During vacation, what was the weather like?

____

____

Listen closely. What 3 nature sounds can you hear?

1 _______________________________

2 _______________________________

3 _______________________________

Look around. What 3 animals or insects do you see?

1 _______________________________

2 _______________________________

3 _______________________________

Did you see a body of water? What was it like?

____

____

Did you see buildings or houses? What were they like?

____

____

____

What is unique about this vacation?

What were the top 5 activities you did in the national park?

1 _______________________________

2 _______________________________

3 _______________________________

4 _______________________________

5 _______________________________

Paste, draw, doodle or write evidence of your exploration here:

JOURNAL WRITING

MY VACATION IN...

OVERALL RATING:

Tell us a story abour your vacation. WHEN did you go on your trip? WHERE did you visit? WHO were you with? WHAT did you do?

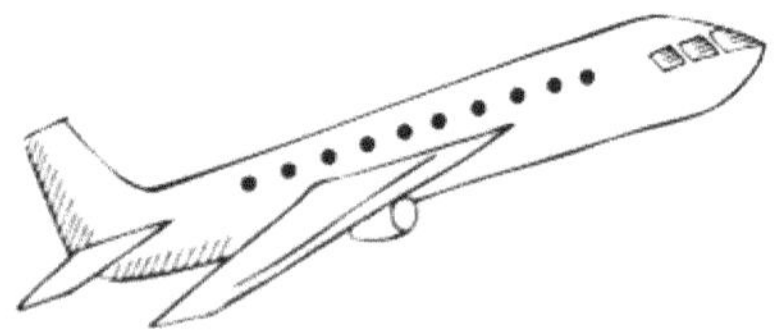

MY EXPLORATION REPORT:

During vacation, what was the weather like?

____

____

Listen closely. What 3 nature sounds can you hear?

1 ___________________________

2 ___________________________

3 ___________________________

Look around. What 3 animals or insects do you see?

1 ___________________________

2 ___________________________

3 ___________________________

Did you see a body of water? What was it like?

____

____

Did you see buildings or houses? What were they like?

____

____

____

What is unique about this vacation?

What were the top 5 activities you did in the national park?

1 ___________________________

2 ___________________________

3 ___________________________

4 ___________________________

5 ___________________________

Paste, draw, doodle or write evidence of your exploration here:

JOURNAL WRITING

MY VACATION IN...

OVERALL RATING:

Tell us a story abour your vacation. WHEN did you go on your trip? WHERE did you visit? WHO were you with? WHAT did you do?

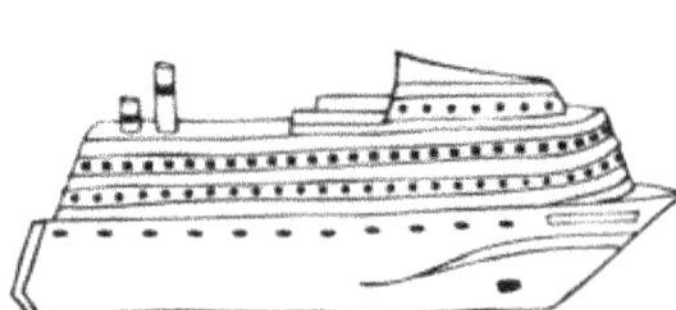

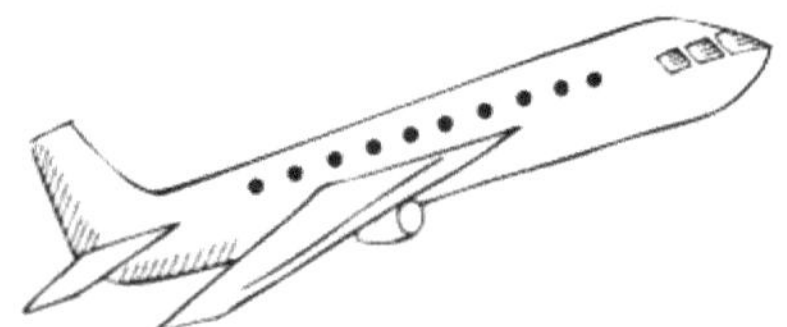

MY EXPLORATION REPORT:

During vacation, what was the weather like?

Listen closely. What 3 nature sounds can you hear?

1
2
3

Look around. What 3 animals or insects do you see?

1
2
3

Did you see a body of water? What was it like?

Did you see buildings or houses? What were they like?

What is unique about this vacation?

What were the top 5 activities you did in the national park?

1
2
3
4
5

Paste, draw, doodle or write evidence of your exploration here:

JOURNAL WRITING

MY VACATION IN...

OVERALL RATING:

Tell us a story abour your vacation. WHEN did you go on your trip? WHERE did you visit? WHO were you with? WHAT did you do?

  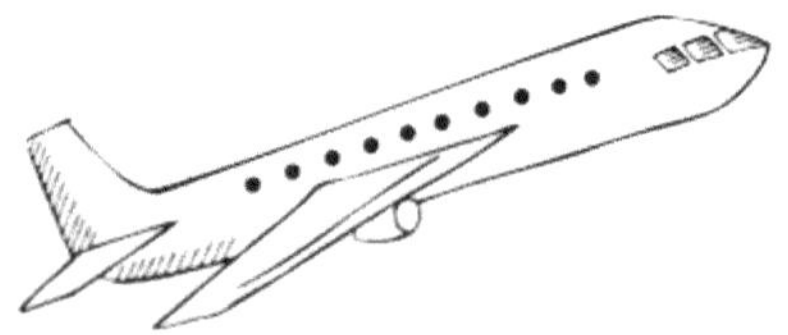

MY EXPLORATION REPORT:

During vacation, what was the weather like?

Listen closely. What 3 nature sounds can you hear?

1
2
3

Look around. What 3 animals or insects do you see?

1
2
3

Did you see a body of water? What was it like?

Did you see buildings or houses? What were they like?

What is unique about this vacation?

What were the top 5 activities you did in the national park?

1
2
3
4
5

Paste, draw, doodle or write evidence of your exploration here:

JOURNAL WRITING

MY VACATION IN...

OVERALL RATING:

Tell us a story abour your vacation. WHEN did you go on your trip? WHERE did you visit? WHO were you with? WHAT did you do?

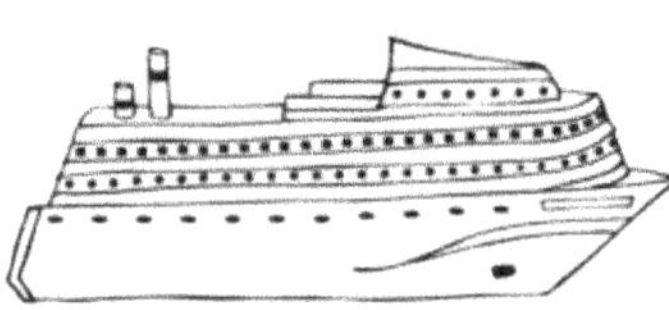

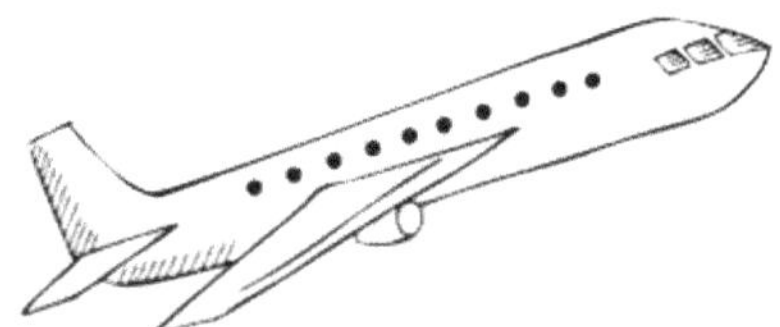

MY EXPLORATION REPORT:

During vacation, what was the weather like?

____

____

Listen closely. What 3 nature sounds can you hear?	Look around. What 3 animals or insects do you see?
1	1
2	2
3	3

Did you see a body of water? What was it like?

____

____

Did you see buildings or houses? What were they like?

____

____

____

What is unique about this vacation?

What were the top 5 activities you did in the national park?

1 _______________________________

2 _______________________________

3 _______________________________

4 _______________________________

5 _______________________________

Paste, draw, doodle or write evidence of your exploration here:

JOURNAL WRITING

MY VACATION IN...

OVERALL RATING:

Tell us a story abour your vacation. WHEN did you go on your trip? WHERE did you visit? WHO were you with? WHAT did you do?

  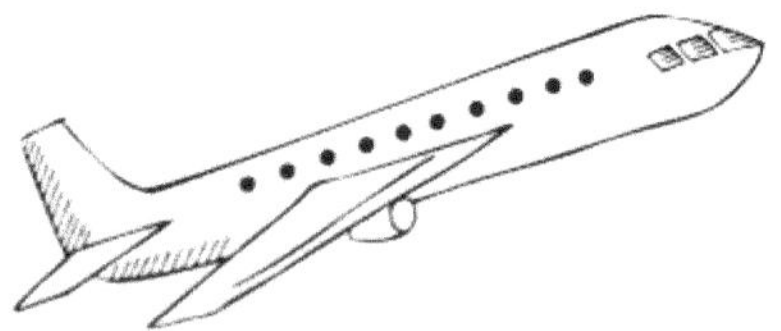

MY EXPLORATION REPORT:

During vacation, what was the weather like?

____

____

Listen closely. What 3 nature sounds can you hear?

1 _______________________

2 _______________________

3 _______________________

Look around. What 3 animals or insects do you see?

1 _______________________

2 _______________________

3 _______________________

Did you see a body of water? What was it like?

____

____

Did you see buildings or houses? What were they like?

____

____

____

What is unique about this vacation?

What were the top 5 activities you did in the national park?

1 _______________________

2 _______________________

3 _______________________

4 _______________________

5 _______________________

Paste, draw, doodle or write evidence of your exploration here:

JOURNAL WRITING

MY VACATION IN...

OVERALL RATING:

Tell us a story abour your vacation. WHEN did you go on your trip? WHERE did you visit? WHO were you with? WHAT did you do?

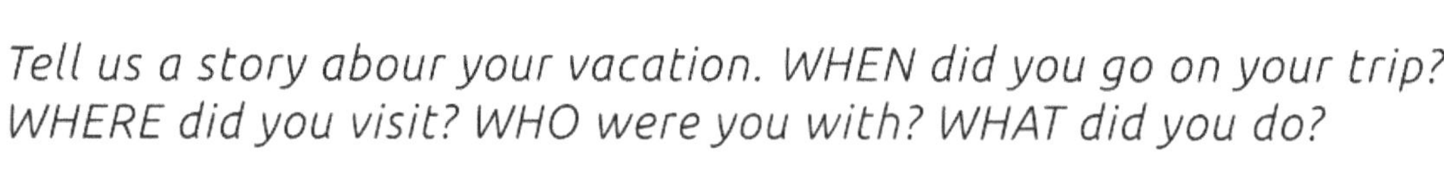

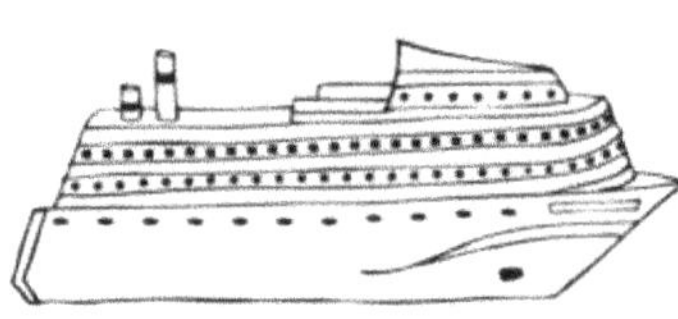

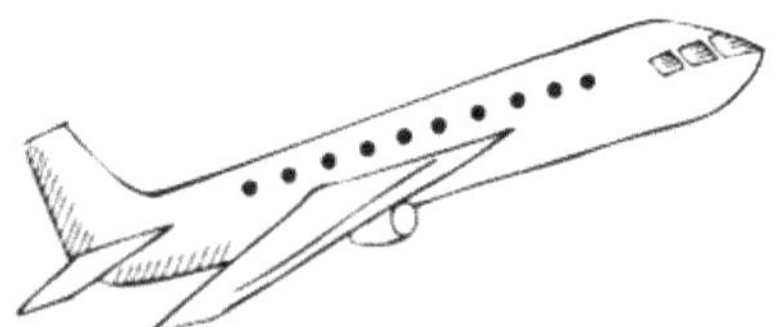

MY EXPLORATION REPORT:

During vacation, what was the weather like?

Listen closely. What 3 nature sounds can you hear?

1

2

3

Look around. What 3 animals or insects do you see?

1

2

3

Did you see a body of water? What was it like?

Did you see buildings or houses? What were they like?

What is unique about this vacation?

What were the top 5 activities you did in the national park?

1

2

3

4

5

Paste, draw, doodle or write evidence of your exploration here:

JOURNAL WRITING

MY VACATION IN...

OVERALL RATING:

Tell us a story abour your vacation. WHEN did you go on your trip? WHERE did you visit? WHO were you with? WHAT did you do?

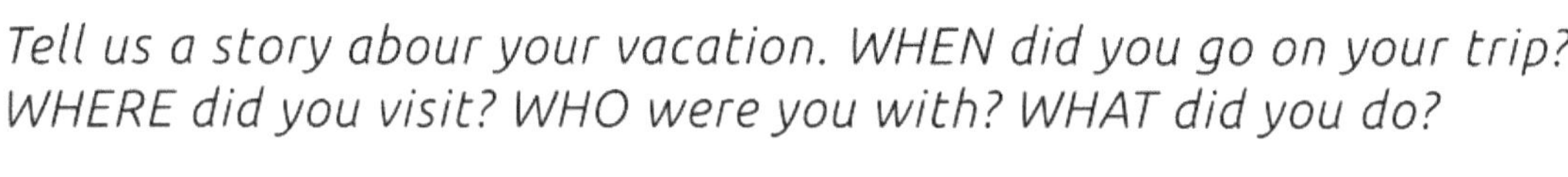

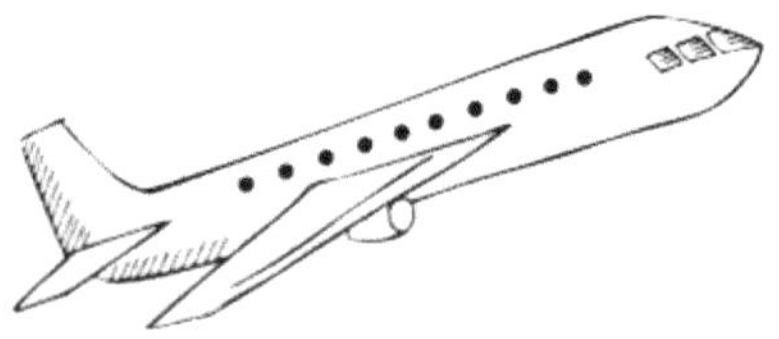

MY EXPLORATION REPORT:

During vacation, what was the weather like?

Listen closely. What 3 nature sounds can you hear?

1
2
3

Look around. What 3 animals or insects do you see?

1
2
3

Did you see a body of water? What was it like?

Did you see buildings or houses? What were they like?

What is unique about this vacation?

What were the top 5 activities you did in the national park?

1
2
3
4
5

Paste, draw, doodle or write evidence of your exploration here:

JOURNAL WRITING

MY VACATION IN...

OVERALL RATING:

Tell us a story abour your vacation. WHEN did you go on your trip? WHERE did you visit? WHO were you with? WHAT did you do?

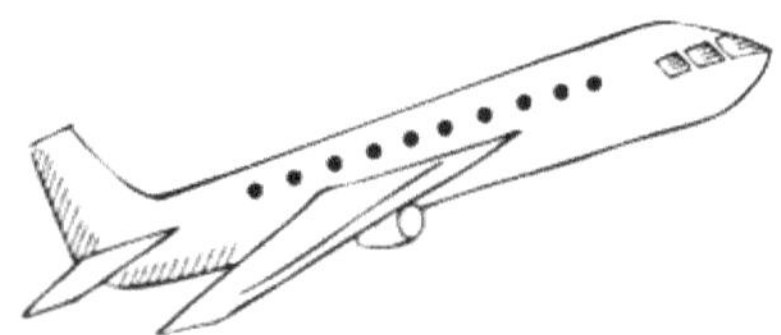

MY EXPLORATION REPORT:

During vacation, what was the weather like?

____

____

Listen closely. What 3 nature sounds can you hear?

1 ______________________________

2 ______________________________

3 ______________________________

Look around. What 3 animals or insects do you see?

1 ______________________________

2 ______________________________

3 ______________________________

Did you see a body of water? What was it like?

____

____

Did you see buildings or houses? What were they like?

____

____

____

What is unique about this vacation?

What were the top 5 activities you did in the national park?

1 ______________________________

2 ______________________________

3 ______________________________

4 ______________________________

5 ______________________________

Paste, draw, doodle or write evidence of your exploration here:

JOURNAL WRITING

MY VACATION IN...

OVERALL RATING:

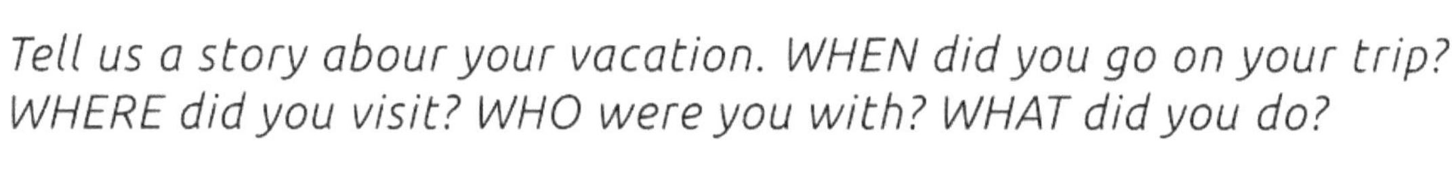

Tell us a story abour your vacation. WHEN did you go on your trip? WHERE did you visit? WHO were you with? WHAT did you do?

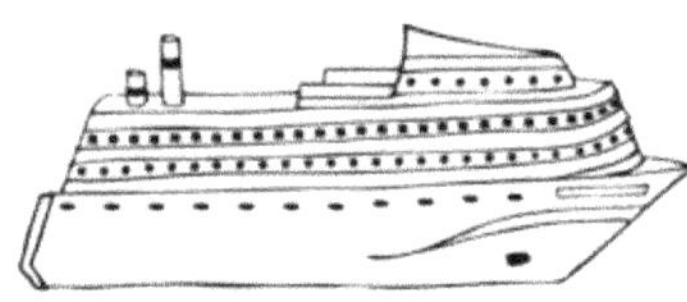

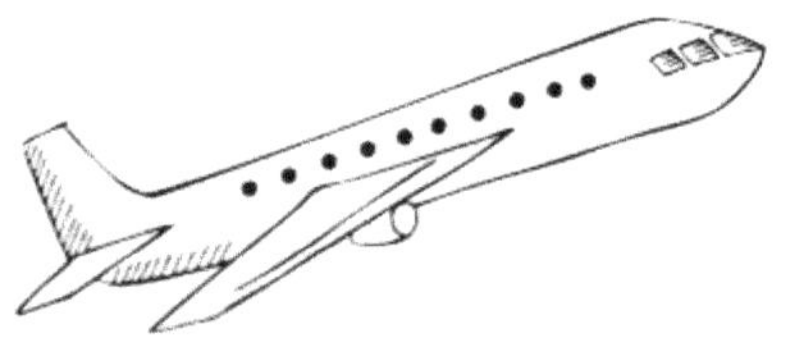

MY EXPLORATION REPORT:

During vacation, what was the weather like?

____

____

Listen closely. What 3 nature sounds can you hear?

1 ___________________________

2 ___________________________

3 ___________________________

Look around. What 3 animals or insects do you see?

1 ___________________________

2 ___________________________

3 ___________________________

Did you see a body of water? What was it like?

____

____

Did you see buildings or houses? What were they like?

____

____

____

What is unique about this vacation?

What were the top 5 activities you did in the national park?

1 ___________________________

2 ___________________________

3 ___________________________

4 ___________________________

5 ___________________________

Paste, draw, doodle or write evidence of your exploration here:

JOURNAL WRITING

MY VACATION IN...

OVERALL RATING:

Tell us a story abour your vacation. WHEN did you go on your trip? WHERE did you visit? WHO were you with? WHAT did you do?

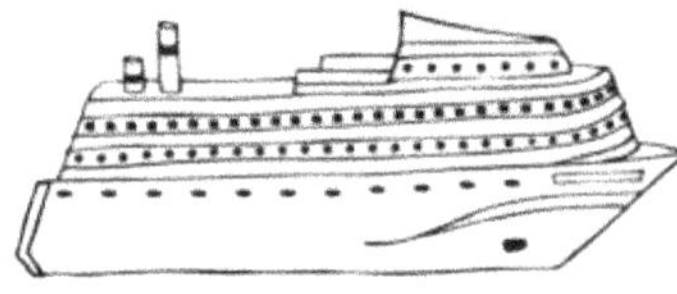

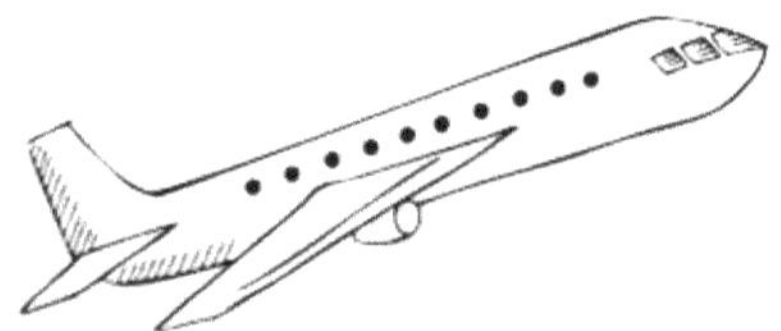

MY EXPLORATION REPORT:

During vacation, what was the weather like?

____

____

Listen closely. What 3 nature sounds can you hear?

1 ____________________________

2 ____________________________

3 ____________________________

Look around. What 3 animals or insects do you see?

1 ____________________________

2 ____________________________

3 ____________________________

Did you see a body of water? What was it like?

____

____

Did you see buildings or houses? What were they like?

____

____

____

What is unique about this vacation?

What were the top 5 activities you did in the national park?

1 ____________________________

2 ____________________________

3 ____________________________

4 ____________________________

5 ____________________________

Paste, draw, doodle or write evidence of your exploration here:

JOURNAL WRITING

MY VACATION IN...

OVERALL RATING:

Tell us a story abour your vacation. WHEN did you go on your trip? WHERE did you visit? WHO were you with? WHAT did you do?

  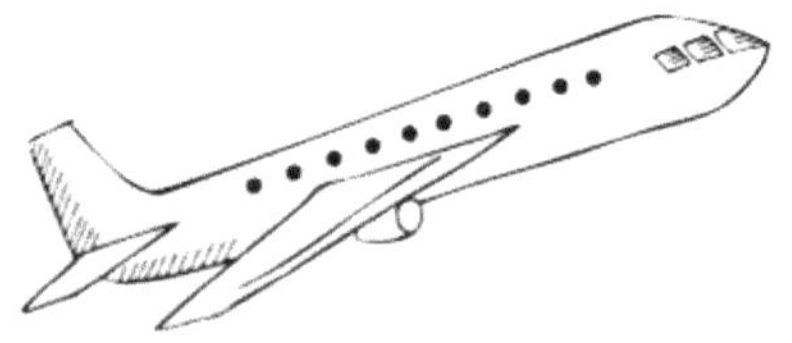

MY EXPLORATION REPORT:

During vacation, what was the weather like?

____

____

Listen closely. What 3 nature sounds can you hear?

1 _______________________

2 _______________________

3 _______________________

Look around. What 3 animals or insects do you see?

1 _______________________

2 _______________________

3 _______________________

Did you see a body of water? What was it like?

____

____

Did you see buildings or houses? What were they like?

____

____

____

What is unique about this vacation?

What were the top 5 activities you did in the national park?

1 _______________________

2 _______________________

3 _______________________

4 _______________________

5 _______________________

Paste, draw, doodle or write evidence of your exploration here:

JOURNAL WRITING

MY VACATION IN...

OVERALL RATING:

Tell us a story abour your vacation. WHEN did you go on your trip? WHERE did you visit? WHO were you with? WHAT did you do?

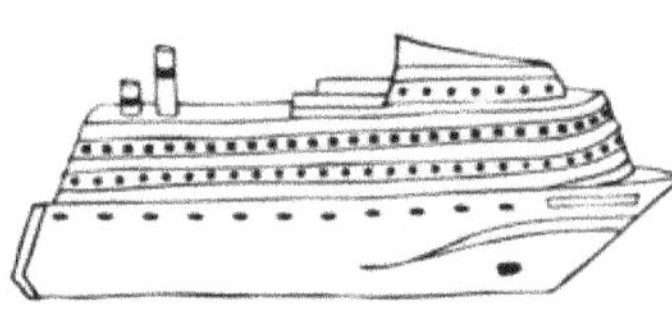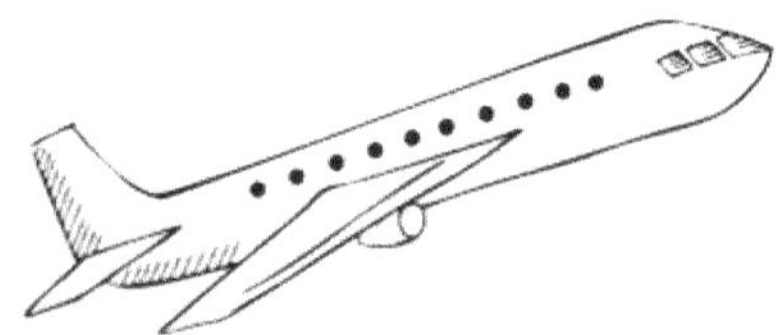

MY EXPLORATION REPORT:

During vacation, what was the weather like?

____

____

Listen closely. What 3 nature sounds can you hear?

1 _______________________

2 _______________________

3 _______________________

Look around. What 3 animals or insects do you see?

1 _______________________

2 _______________________

3 _______________________

Did you see a body of water? What was it like?

____

____

Did you see buildings or houses? What were they like?

____

____

____

What is unique about this vacation?

What were the top 5 activities you did in the national park?

1 _______________________

2 _______________________

3 _______________________

4 _______________________

5 _______________________

Paste, draw, doodle or write evidence of your exploration here:

JOURNAL WRITING

MY VACATION IN...

OVERALL RATING:

Tell us a story abour your vacation. WHEN did you go on your trip? WHERE did you visit? WHO were you with? WHAT did you do?

  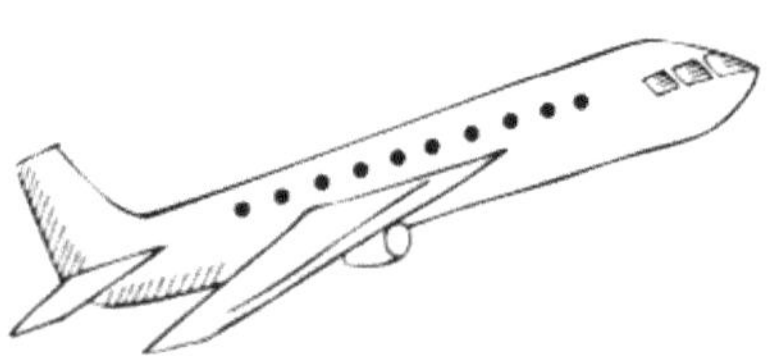

MY EXPLORATION REPORT:

During vacation, what was the weather like?

____

____

Listen closely. What 3 nature sounds can you hear?

1 _______________________________

2 _______________________________

3 _______________________________

Look around. What 3 animals or insects do you see?

1 _______________________________

2 _______________________________

3 _______________________________

Did you see a body of water? What was it like?

____

____

Did you see buildings or houses? What were they like?

____

____

____

What is unique about this vacation?

What were the top 5 activities you did in the national park?

1 _______________________________

2 _______________________________

3 _______________________________

4 _______________________________

5 _______________________________

Paste, draw, doodle or write evidence of your exploration here:

JOURNAL WRITING

MY VACATION IN...

OVERALL RATING:

Tell us a story abour your vacation. WHEN did you go on your trip? WHERE did you visit? WHO were you with? WHAT did you do?

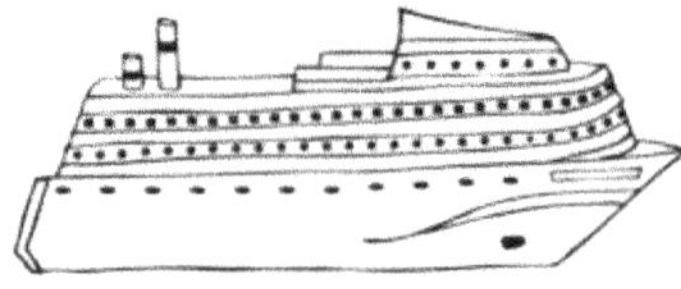  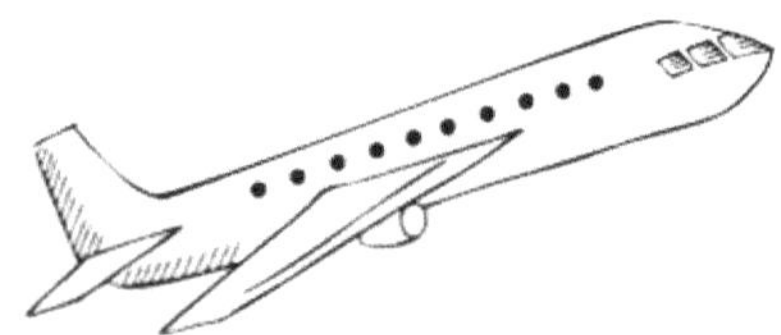

MY EXPLORATION REPORT:

During vacation, what was the weather like?

____

____

Listen closely. What 3 nature sounds can you hear?

1 ___________________________

2 ___________________________

3 ___________________________

Look around. What 3 animals or insects do you see?

1 ___________________________

2 ___________________________

3 ___________________________

Did you see a body of water? What was it like?

____

____

Did you see buildings or houses? What were they like?

____

____

What is unique about this vacation?

What were the top 5 activities you did in the national park?

1 ___________________________

2 ___________________________

3 ___________________________

4 ___________________________

5 ___________________________

Paste, draw, doodle or write evidence of your exploration here:

JOURNAL WRITING

MY VACATION IN...

OVERALL RATING:

Tell us a story abour your vacation. WHEN did you go on your trip? WHERE did you visit? WHO were you with? WHAT did you do?

  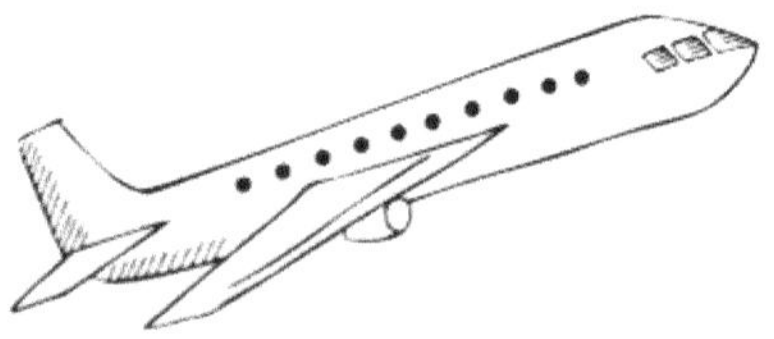

MY EXPLORATION REPORT:

During vacation, what was the weather like?

Listen closely. What 3 nature sounds can you hear?

1
2
3

Look around. What 3 animals or insects do you see?

1
2
3

Did you see a body of water? What was it like?

Did you see buildings or houses? What were they like?

What is unique about this vacation?

What were the top 5 activities you did in the national park?

1
2
3
4
5

Paste, draw, doodle or write evidence of your exploration here:

JOURNAL WRITING

MY VACATION IN...

OVERALL RATING:

Tell us a story abour your vacation. WHEN did you go on your trip? WHERE did you visit? WHO were you with? WHAT did you do?

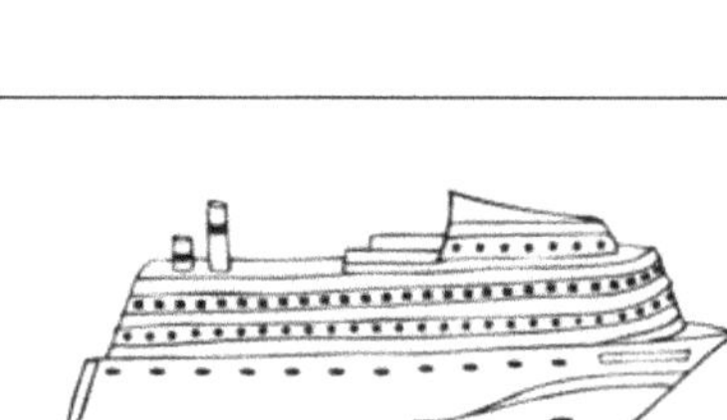  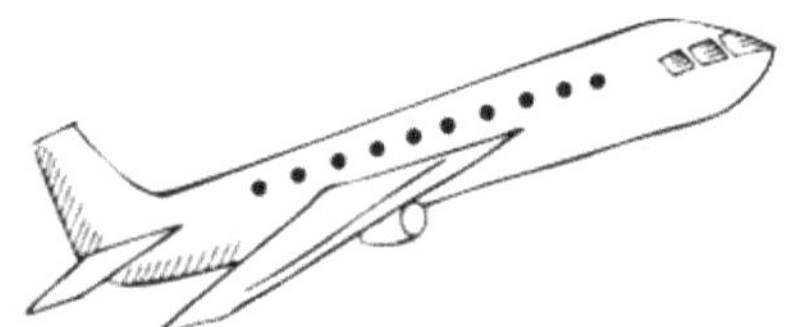

MY EXPLORATION REPORT:

During vacation, what was the weather like?

Listen closely. What 3 nature sounds can you hear?

1

2

3

Look around. What 3 animals or insects do you see?

1

2

3

Did you see a body of water? What was it like?

Did you see buildings or houses? What were they like?

What is unique about this vacation?

What were the top 5 activities you did in the national park?

1

2

3

4

5

Paste, draw, doodle or write evidence of your exploration here:

JOURNAL WRITING

MY VACATION IN...

OVERALL RATING:

Tell us a story abour your vacation. WHEN did you go on your trip? WHERE did you visit? WHO were you with? WHAT did you do?

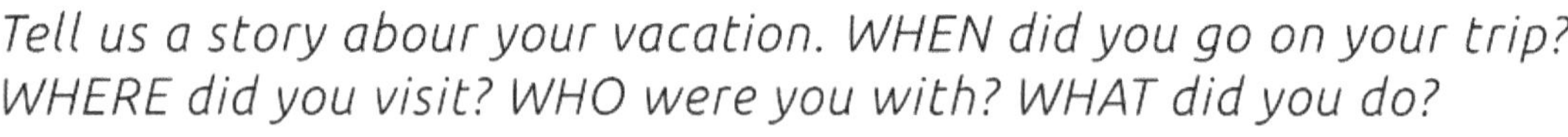

MY EXPLORATION REPORT:

During vacation, what was the weather like?

Listen closely. What 3 nature sounds can you hear?

1
2
3

Look around. What 3 animals or insects do you see?

1
2
3

Did you see a body of water? What was it like?

Did you see buildings or houses? What were they like?

What is unique about this vacation?

What were the top 5 activities you did in the national park?

1
2
3
4
5

Paste, draw, doodle or write evidence of your exploration here:

JOURNAL WRITING

MY VACATION IN...

OVERALL RATING:

Tell us a story abour your vacation. WHEN did you go on your trip? WHERE did you visit? WHO were you with? WHAT did you do?

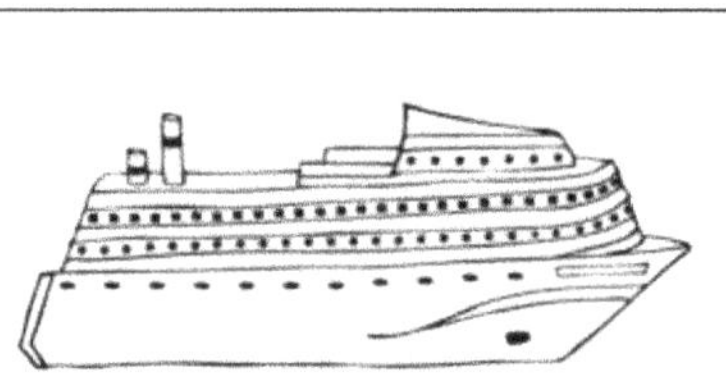  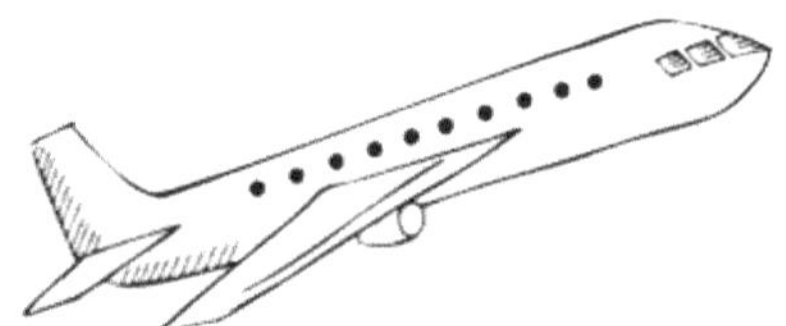

MY EXPLORATION REPORT:

During vacation, what was the weather like?

____

____

Listen closely. What 3 nature sounds can you hear?

1 _______________________

2 _______________________

3 _______________________

Look around. What 3 animals or insects do you see?

1 _______________________

2 _______________________

3 _______________________

Did you see a body of water? What was it like?

____

____

Did you see buildings or houses? What were they like?

____

____

What is unique about this vacation?

What were the top 5 activities you did in the national park?

1 _______________________

2 _______________________

3 _______________________

4 _______________________

5 _______________________

Paste, draw, doodle or write evidence of your exploration here:

JOURNAL WRITING

MY VACATION IN...

OVERALL RATING:

Tell us a story abour your vacation. WHEN did you go on your trip? WHERE did you visit? WHO were you with? WHAT did you do?

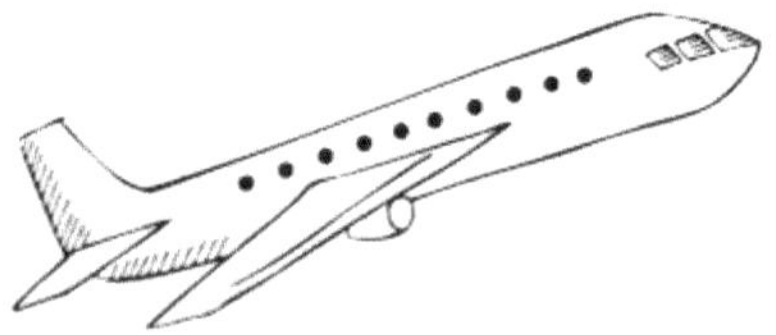

MY EXPLORATION REPORT:

During vacation, what was the weather like?

____

____

Listen closely. What 3 nature sounds can you hear?

1 ___________________________

2 ___________________________

3 ___________________________

Look around. What 3 animals or insects do you see?

1 ___________________________

2 ___________________________

3 ___________________________

Did you see a body of water? What was it like?

____

____

Did you see buildings or houses? What were they like?

____

____

____

What is unique about this vacation?

What were the top 5 activities you did in the national park?

1 ___________________________

2 ___________________________

3 ___________________________

4 ___________________________

5 ___________________________

Paste, draw, doodle or write evidence of your exploration here:

JOURNAL WRITING

MY VACATION IN...

OVERALL RATING:

Tell us a story abour your vacation. WHEN did you go on your trip? WHERE did you visit? WHO were you with? WHAT did you do?

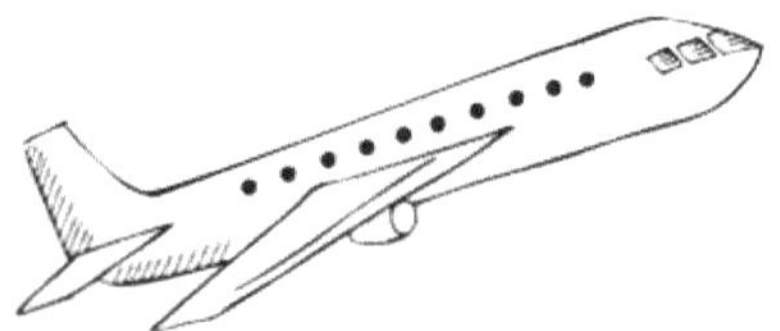

MY EXPLORATION REPORT:

During vacation, what was the weather like?

Listen closely. What 3 nature sounds can you hear?

1
2
3

Look around. What 3 animals or insects do you see?

1
2
3

Did you see a body of water? What was it like?

Did you see buildings or houses? What were they like?

What is unique about this vacation?

What were the top 5 activities you did in the national park?

1
2
3
4
5

Paste, draw, doodle or write evidence of your exploration here:

JOURNAL WRITING

MY VACATION IN...

OVERALL RATING:

Tell us a story abour your vacation. WHEN did you go on your trip? WHERE did you visit? WHO were you with? WHAT did you do?

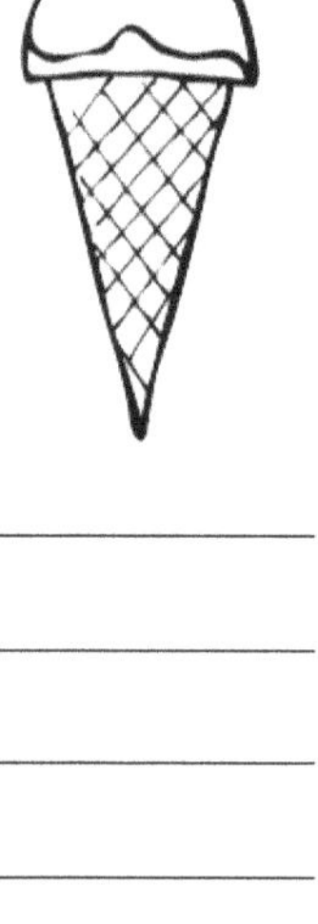

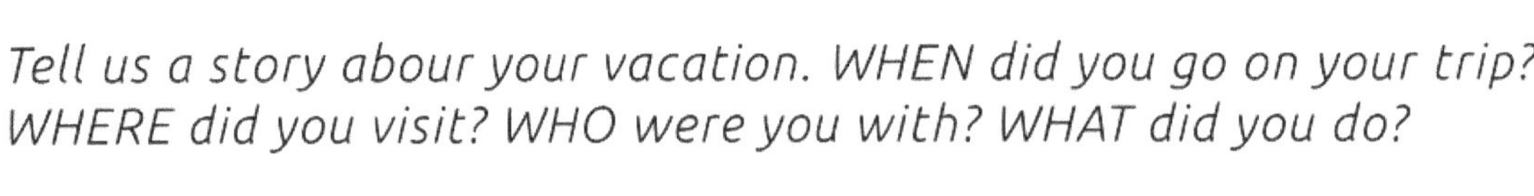

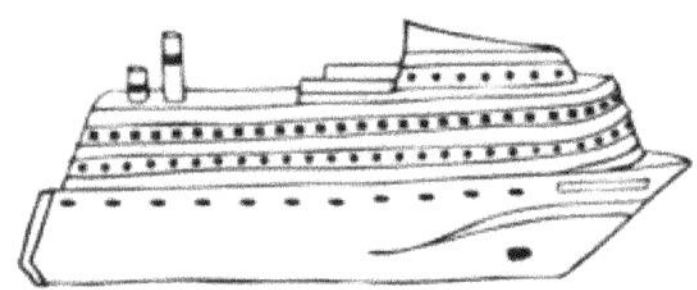

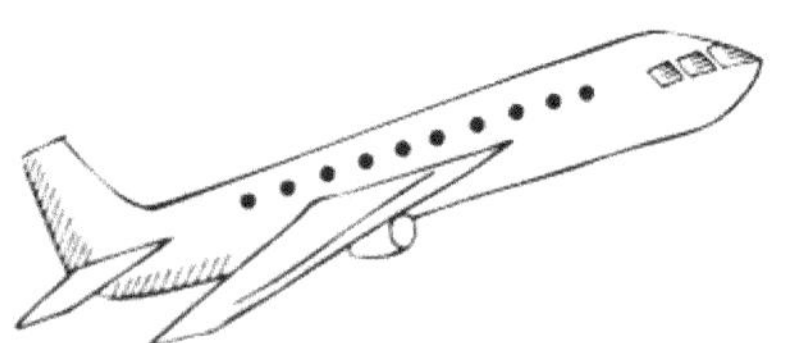

MY EXPLORATION REPORT:

During vacation, what was the weather like?

____

____

Listen closely. What 3 nature sounds can you hear?

1 _____________________________

2 _____________________________

3 _____________________________

Look around. What 3 animals or insects do you see?

1 _____________________________

2 _____________________________

3 _____________________________

Did you see a body of water? What was it like?

____

____

Did you see buildings or houses? What were they like?

____

____

____

What is unique about this vacation?

What were the top 5 activities you did in the national park?

1 _____________________________

2 _____________________________

3 _____________________________

4 _____________________________

5 _____________________________

Paste, draw, doodle or write evidence of your exploration here:

JOURNAL WRITING

MY VACATION IN...

OVERALL RATING:

Tell us a story abour your vacation. WHEN did you go on your trip? WHERE did you visit? WHO were you with? WHAT did you do?

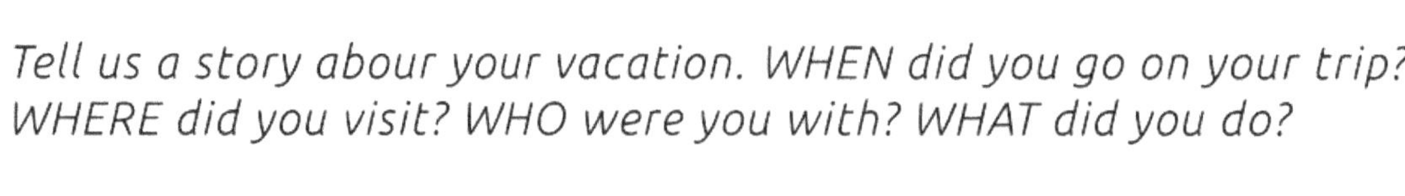

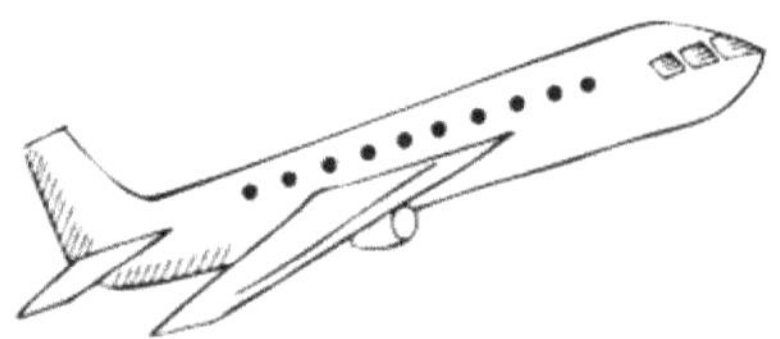

MY EXPLORATION REPORT:

During vacation, what was the weather like?

Listen closely. What 3 nature sounds can you hear?

1

2

3

Look around. What 3 animals or insects do you see?

1

2

3

Did you see a body of water? What was it like?

Did you see buildings or houses? What were they like?

What is unique about this vacation?

What were the top 5 activities you did in the national park?

1

2

3

4

5

Paste, draw, doodle or write evidence of your exploration here:

JOURNAL WRITING

MY VACATION IN...

OVERALL RATING:

Tell us a story abour your vacation. WHEN did you go on your trip? WHERE did you visit? WHO were you with? WHAT did you do?

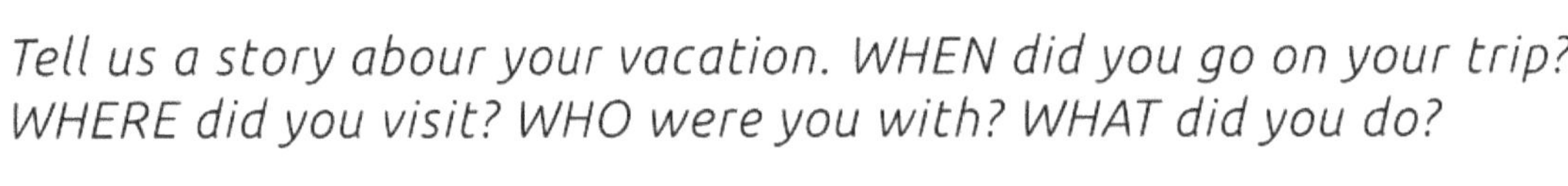

  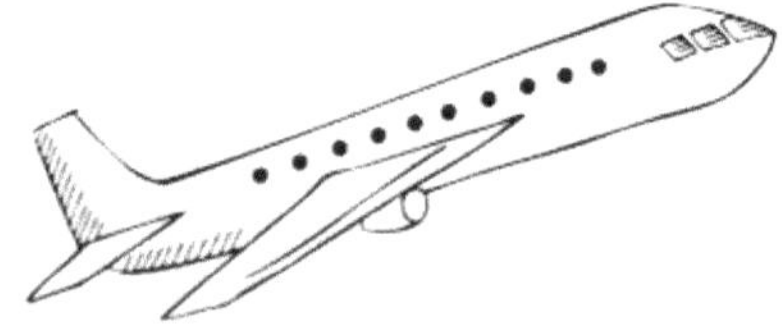

MY EXPLORATION REPORT:

During vacation, what was the weather like?

____

____

Listen closely. What 3 nature sounds can you hear?

1 ___________________________

2 ___________________________

3 ___________________________

Look around. What 3 animals or insects do you see?

1 ___________________________

2 ___________________________

3 ___________________________

Did you see a body of water? What was it like?

____

____

Did you see buildings or houses? What were they like?

____

____

____

What is unique about this vacation?

What were the top 5 activities you did in the national park?

1 ___________________________

2 ___________________________

3 ___________________________

4 ___________________________

5 ___________________________

Paste, draw, doodle or write evidence of your exploration here:

JOURNAL WRITING

MY VACATION IN...

OVERALL RATING:

Tell us a story abour your vacation. WHEN did you go on your trip? WHERE did you visit? WHO were you with? WHAT did you do?

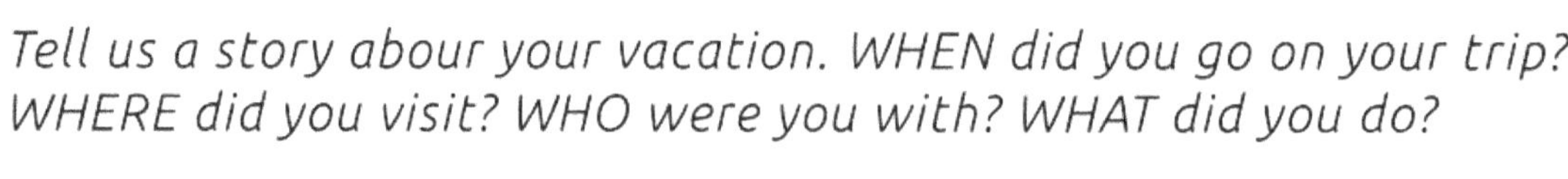

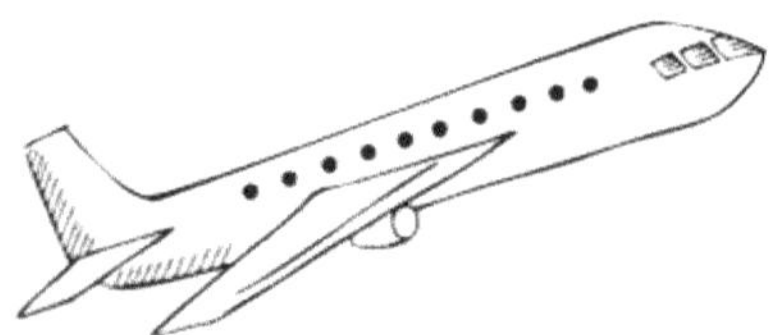

MY EXPLORATION REPORT:

During vacation, what was the weather like?

____

____

Listen closely. What 3 nature sounds can you hear?

1 ______________________________

2 ______________________________

3 ______________________________

Look around. What 3 animals or insects do you see?

1 ______________________________

2 ______________________________

3 ______________________________

Did you see a body of water? What was it like?

____

____

Did you see buildings or houses? What were they like?

____

____

____

What is unique about this vacation?

What were the top 5 activities you did in the national park?

1 ______________________________

2 ______________________________

3 ______________________________

4 ______________________________

5 ______________________________

Paste, draw, doodle or write evidence of your exploration here:

JOURNAL WRITING

MY VACATION IN...

OVERALL RATING:

Tell us a story abour your vacation. WHEN did you go on your trip? WHERE did you visit? WHO were you with? WHAT did you do?

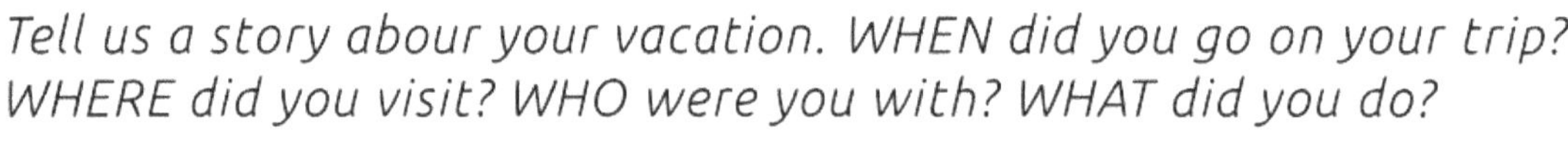

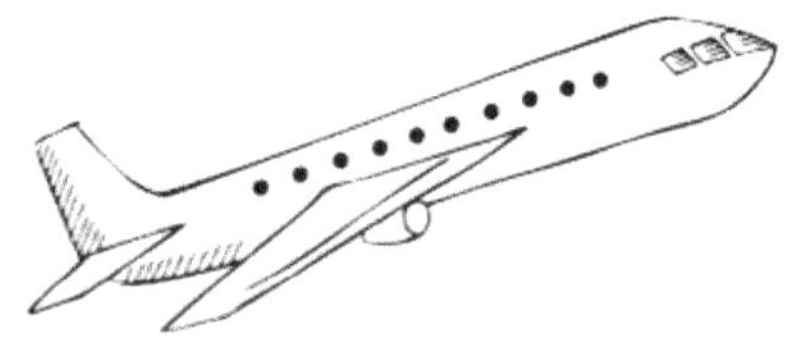

MY EXPLORATION REPORT:

During vacation, what was the weather like?

____

____

Listen closely. What 3 nature sounds can you hear?

1 _______________________

2 _______________________

3 _______________________

Look around. What 3 animals or insects do you see?

1 _______________________

2 _______________________

3 _______________________

Did you see a body of water? What was it like?

____

____

Did you see buildings or houses? What were they like?

____

____

____

What is unique about this vacation?

What were the top 5 activities you did in the national park?

1 _______________________

2 _______________________

3 _______________________

4 _______________________

5 _______________________

Paste, draw, doodle or write evidence of your exploration here:

JOURNAL WRITING

MY VACATION IN...

OVERALL RATING:

Tell us a story abour your vacation. WHEN did you go on your trip? WHERE did you visit? WHO were you with? WHAT did you do?

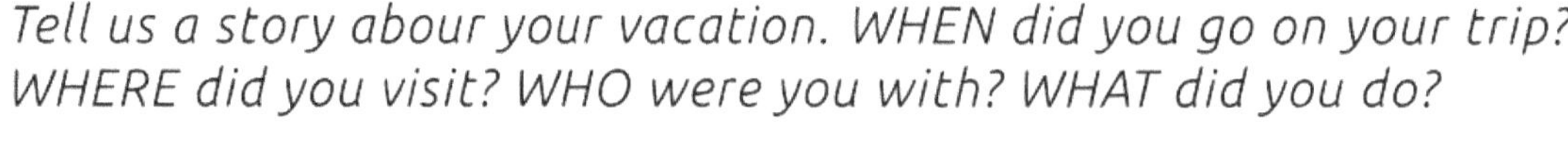

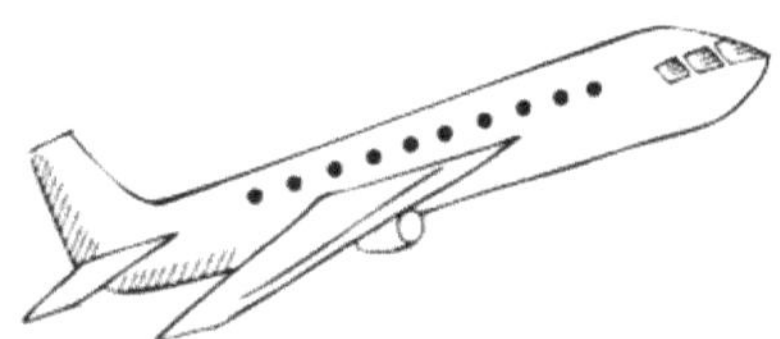

MY EXPLORATION REPORT:

During vacation, what was the weather like?

____

____

Listen closely. What 3 nature sounds can you hear?

1 _____________________________

2 _____________________________

3 _____________________________

Look around. What 3 animals or insects do you see?

1 _____________________________

2 _____________________________

3 _____________________________

Did you see a body of water? What was it like?

____

____

Did you see buildings or houses? What were they like?

____

____

____

What is unique about this vacation?

What were the top 5 activities you did in the national park?

1 _____________________________

2 _____________________________

3 _____________________________

4 _____________________________

5 _____________________________

Paste, draw, doodle or write evidence of your exploration here:

JOURNAL WRITING

MY VACATION IN...

OVERALL RATING:

Tell us a story abour your vacation. WHEN did you go on your trip? WHERE did you visit? WHO were you with? WHAT did you do?

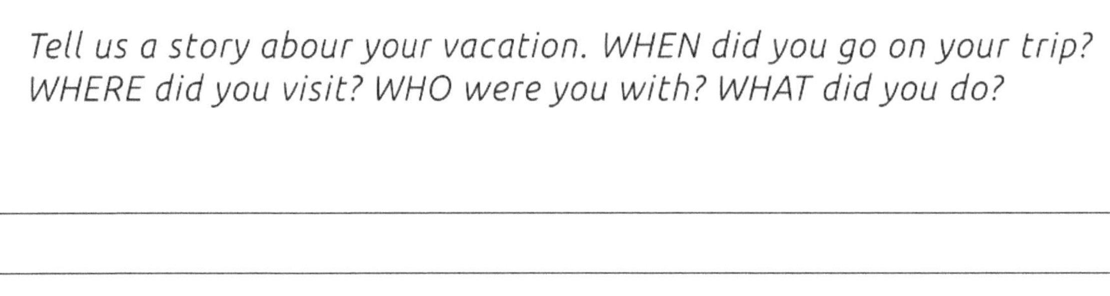

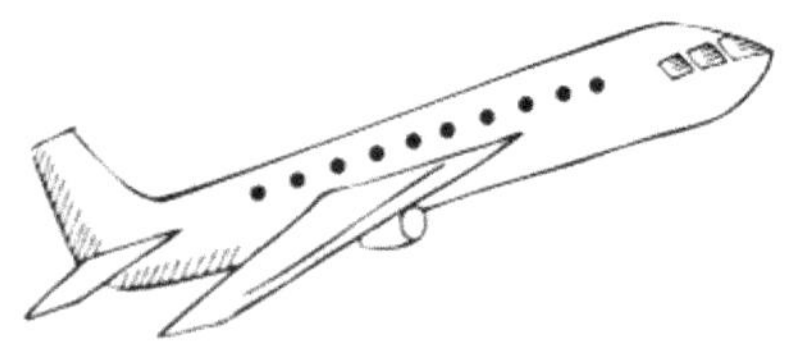

MY EXPLORATION REPORT:

During vacation, what was the weather like?

Listen closely. What 3 nature sounds can you hear?

1

2

3

Look around. What 3 animals or insects do you see?

1

2

3

Did you see a body of water? What was it like?

Did you see buildings or houses? What were they like?

What is unique about this vacation?

What were the top 5 activities you did in the national park?

1

2

3

4

5

Paste, draw, doodle or write evidence of your exploration here:

JOURNAL WRITING

MY VACATION IN...

OVERALL RATING:

Tell us a story abour your vacation. WHEN did you go on your trip? WHERE did you visit? WHO were you with? WHAT did you do?

  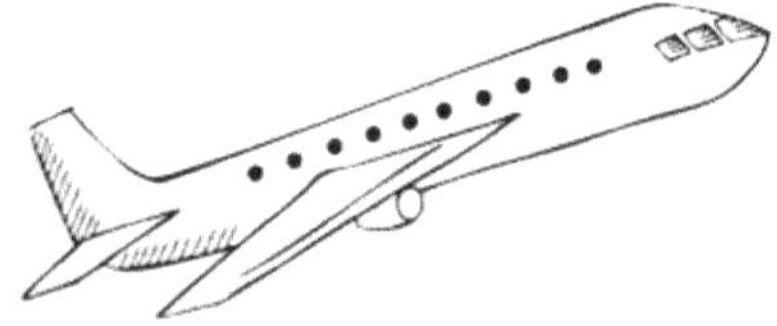

MY EXPLORATION REPORT:

During vacation, what was the weather like?

____

____

Listen closely. What 3 nature sounds can you hear?

1 _______________________________

2 _______________________________

3 _______________________________

Look around. What 3 animals or insects do you see?

1 _______________________________

2 _______________________________

3 _______________________________

Did you see a body of water? What was it like?

____

____

Did you see buildings or houses? What were they like?

____

____

____

What is unique about this vacation?

What were the top 5 activities you did in the national park?

1 _______________________________

2 _______________________________

3 _______________________________

4 _______________________________

5 _______________________________

Paste, draw, doodle or write evidence of your exploration here:

JOURNAL WRITING

MY VACATION IN...

OVERALL RATING:

Tell us a story abour your vacation. WHEN did you go on your trip? WHERE did you visit? WHO were you with? WHAT did you do?

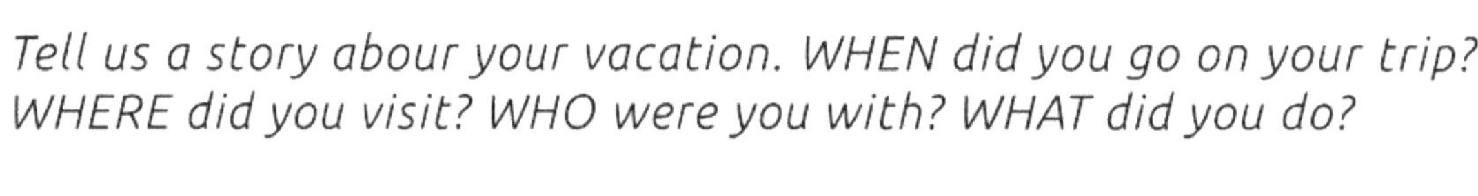

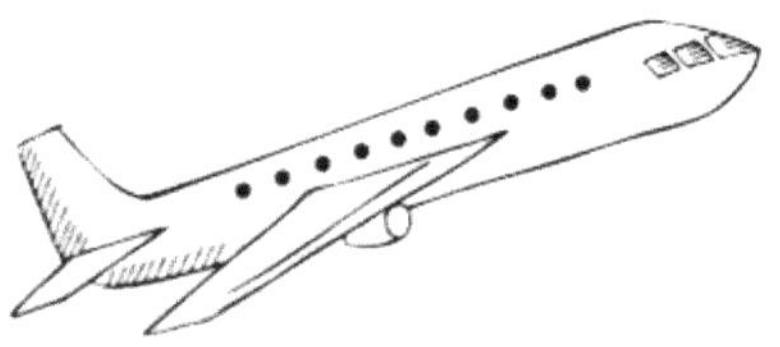

MY EXPLORATION REPORT:

During vacation, what was the weather like?

Listen closely. What 3 nature sounds can you hear?

1
2
3

Look around. What 3 animals or insects do you see?

1
2
3

Did you see a body of water? What was it like?

Did you see buildings or houses? What were they like?

What is unique about this vacation?

What were the top 5 activities you did in the national park?

1
2
3
4
5

Paste, draw, doodle or write evidence of your exploration here:

JOURNAL WRITING

MY VACATION IN...

OVERALL RATING:

Tell us a story abour your vacation. WHEN did you go on your trip? WHERE did you visit? WHO were you with? WHAT did you do?

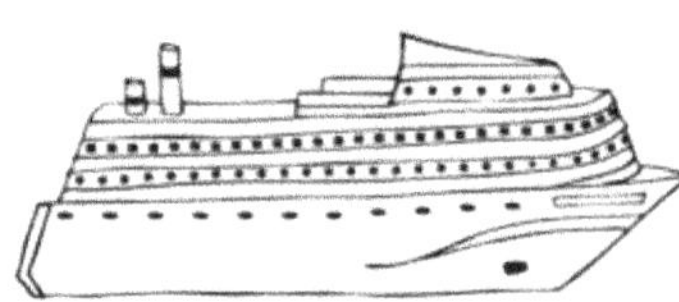  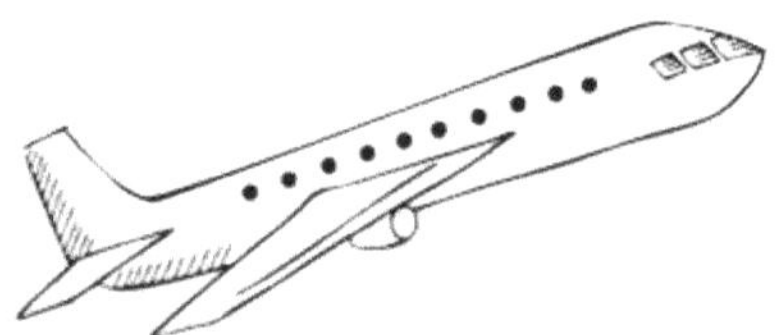

MY EXPLORATION REPORT:

During vacation, what was the weather like?

____

____

Listen closely. What 3 nature sounds can you hear?

1 ___________________________

2 ___________________________

3 ___________________________

Look around. What 3 animals or insects do you see?

1 ___________________________

2 ___________________________

3 ___________________________

Did you see a body of water? What was it like?

____

____

Did you see buildings or houses? What were they like?

____

____

____

What is unique about this vacation?

What were the top 5 activities you did in the national park?

1 ___________________________

2 ___________________________

3 ___________________________

4 ___________________________

5 ___________________________

Paste, draw, doodle or write evidence of your exploration here:

SCRAPBOOKING

Use these pages to sketch, doodle, or paste keepsakes like photos, tickets, stamps, leaves or other things to remember your vacations by.

SCRAPBOOKING

Use these pages to sketch, doodle, or paste keepsakes like photos, tickets, stamps, leaves or other things to remember your vacations by.

SCRAPBOOKING

Use these pages to sketch, doodle, or paste keepsakes like photos, tickets, stamps, leaves or other things to remember your vacations by.

SCRAPBOOKING

Use these pages to sketch, doodle, or paste keepsakes like photos, tickets, stamps, leaves or other things to remember your vacations by.

SCRAPBOOKING

Use these pages to sketch, doodle, or paste keepsakes like photos, tickets, stamps, leaves or other things to remember your vacations by.

SCRAPBOOKING

Use these pages to sketch, doodle, or paste keepsakes like photos, tickets, stamps, leaves or other things to remember your vacations by.

SCRAPBOOKING

Use these pages to sketch, doodle, or paste keepsakes like photos, tickets, stamps, leaves or other things to remember your vacations by.

SCRAPBOOKING

Use these pages to sketch, doodle, or paste keepsakes like photos, tickets, stamps, leaves or other things to remember your vacations by.

SCRAPBOOKING

Use these pages to sketch, doodle, or paste keepsakes like photos, tickets, stamps, leaves or other things to remember your vacations by.

SCRAPBOOKING

Use these pages to sketch, doodle, or paste keepsakes like photos, tickets, stamps, leaves or other things to remember your vacations by.

SCRAPBOOKING

Use these pages to sketch, doodle, or paste keepsakes like photos, tickets, stamps, leaves or other things to remember your vacations by.

SCRAPBOOKING

Use these pages to sketch, doodle, or paste keepsakes like photos, tickets, stamps, leaves or other things to remember your vacations by.

SCRAPBOOKING

Use these pages to sketch, doodle, or paste keepsakes like photos, tickets, stamps, leaves or other things to remember your vacations by.

SCRAPBOOKING

Use these pages to sketch, doodle, or paste keepsakes like photos, tickets, stamps, leaves or other things to remember your vacations by.

SCRAPBOOKING

Use these pages to sketch, doodle, or paste keepsakes like photos, tickets, stamps, leaves or other things to remember your vacations by.

SCRAPBOOKING

Use these pages to sketch, doodle, or paste keepsakes like photos, tickets, stamps, leaves or other things to remember your vacations by.

SCRAPBOOKING

Use these pages to sketch, doodle, or paste keepsakes like photos, tickets, stamps, leaves or other things to remember your vacations by.

SCRAPBOOKING

Use these pages to sketch, doodle, or paste keepsakes like photos, tickets, stamps, leaves or other things to remember your vacations by.

SCRAPBOOKING

Use these pages to sketch, doodle, or paste keepsakes like photos, tickets, stamps, leaves or other things to remember your vacations by.

SCRAPBOOKING

Use these pages to sketch, doodle, or paste keepsakes like photos, tickets, stamps, leaves or other things to remember your vacations by.

SCRAPBOOKING

Use these pages to sketch, doodle, or paste keepsakes like photos, tickets, stamps, leaves or other things to remember your vacations by.

SCRAPBOOKING

Use these pages to sketch, doodle, or paste keepsakes like photos, tickets, stamps, leaves or other things to remember your vacations by.

SCRAPBOOKING

Use these pages to sketch, doodle, or paste keepsakes like photos, tickets, stamps, leaves or other things to remember your vacations by.

SCRAPBOOKING

Use these pages to sketch, doodle, or paste keepsakes like photos, tickets, stamps, leaves or other things to remember your vacations by.

SCRAPBOOKING

Use these pages to sketch, doodle, or paste keepsakes like photos, tickets, stamps, leaves or other things to remember your vacations by.

www.ingramcontent.com/pod-product-compliance
Lightning Source LLC
Chambersburg PA
CBHW040145110726
48005CB00018B/2657